HALF
SUN HALF
SLEEP

NEW POEMS

Half Sun Half Sleep
To Mix With Time
A Cage of Spines
Another Animal

HALF SUN HALF SLEEP

NEW POEMS

MAY SWENSON

CHARLES SCRIBNER'S SONS
NEW YORK

Most of the poems collected in *Half Sun Half Sleep* were first published in the following magazines or anthologies:

Arts in Society (University of Wisconsin, Milwaukee), *The Atlantic, Carleton Miscellany* (Carleton College, Northfield, Minn.), *Chelsea, Harper's, Harper's Bazaar, Hudson Review, Stand* (Leeds, England), *Tri-Quarterly* and *Voices No. 2*. Copyright © 1962, 1963, 1964, 1965, 1966 May Swenson.

The following poems appeared first in *The New Yorker:* "Colors Without Objects," "A City Garden in April," "Dear Elizabeth," "Flying Home from Utah," "In a Museum Cabinet," "The Kite," "The Little Rapids," "Out of the Sea, Early," "Rain at Wildwood," "On Handling Some Small Shells from the Windward Islands," "The Wave and the Dune," "A Yellow Circle" and "Naked in Borneo." Copyright © 1963, 1964, 1965, 1966 The New Yorker Magazine, Inc.

The following poems appeared first in anthologies: "3 Models of the Universe" in POETRY IN CRYSTAL (under the title, "Models of the Universe"). Copyright © 1963 Steuben Glass.

"Cause & Effect" in POETRY AND POWER (Basic Books, 1964). Copyright © 1964 Basic Books). "To Make a Play" in THEATRE, NO. 2. Copyright © 1965 Repertory Theatre of Lincoln Center, Inc., and Hill and Wang, Inc.

The translations of poems by six contemporary Swedish poets are part of a project commissioned by the Bollingen Foundation under the auspices of The Poetry Center (New York) and were made with the assistance of Bo Rosenquist, linguist, who furnished literal prose renditions. Sources for the Swedish originals are as follows:

ALL NORDENS LYRIK, Bonniers, Stockholm 1954: "I Rörelse" ("On the Road") by Karin Boye; "Vintersaga" ("Winter Tale") by Werner Aspenström; "Hög Utsikt" ("High View") by Harry Martinson.

ANDRA RITTER, Bonniers, Stockholm 1951: "Innestängd" ("Locked In") by Ingemar Gustafson.

50-TALS LYRIK, Bonniers, Stockholm 1955: "Under En Fallärdig Regnbåge" ("Under a Ramshackle Rainbow") by Ingemar Gustafson.

100 NORDISKA DIKTER, collected by Erik Blomberg, Fib:s Lyrikklub, Stockholm 1961: "En Värld Är Varje Människa" ("Each Man Is a Universe") by Gunnar Ekelöf; "Pastoralsvit III" ("Pastoral Suite III") by Eric Lindegren.

100 SVENSKA DIKTER, collected by Eric Blomberg, Fib:s Lyrikklub, Stockholm 1961: "Ikaros" ("Icarus") by Eric Lindegren; "Hostsejd" ("Autumn Trance") by Gunnar Ekelöf; "Kväll I Inlandet" ("Evening Inland") by Harry Martinson; "Ja Visst Gör Det Ont" ("Yes It Hurts") by Karin Boye.

For J., the first to read this book.

CONTENTS

Poems

HALF
SUN HALF
SLEEP

Poems

AFTER THE DENTIST

My left upper
lip and half

my nose is gone.
I drink my coffee

on the right from
a warped cup

whose left lip dips.
My cigarette's

thick as a finger.
Somebody else's.

I put lip-
stick on a cloth-

stuffed doll's
face that's

surprised when one
side smiles.

AFTER THE FLIGHT OF RANGER VII

Moon
old fossil
to be scrubbed
and studied
like a turtle's stomach

prodded over on your back
Invulnerable hump
that stumped us

pincers prepare to
pick your secrets
bludgeons of light
to force your seams

Old fossil
glistening
in the continuous rain
of meteorites
blown to you from
between the stars
Stilt feet
mobilize to alight upon you
Ticking feelers
determine your fissures

to impact a pest
of electric eggs in the
cracks of your cold
volcanoes
Tycho Copernicus Kappa
look for geysers

strange abrasions
zodiacal wounds

ALL THAT TIME

I saw two trees embracing.
One leaned on the other
as if to throw her down.
But she was the upright one.
Since their twin youth, maybe she
had been pulling him toward her
all that time,

and finally almost uprooted him.
He was the thin, dry, insecure one,
the most wind-warped, you could see.
And where their tops tangled
it looked like he was crying
on her shoulder.
On the other hand, maybe he

had been trying to weaken her,
break her, or at least
make her bend
over backwards for him
just a little bit.
And all that time
she was standing up to him

the best she could.
She was the most stubborn,
the straightest one, that's a fact.
But he had been willing

to change himself—
even if it was for the worse—
all that time.

At the top they looked like one
tree, where they were embracing.
It was plain they'd be
always together.
Too late now to part.
When the wind blew, you could hear
them rubbing on each other.

APRIL LIGHT

Lined with light
the twigs are stubby arrows.
A gilded trunk writhes
upward from the roots,
from the pit of the black tentacles.

In the book of spring
a bare-limbed torso
is the first illustration.

Light teaches the tree
to beget leaves,
to embroider itself all over
with green reality,
until summer becomes
its steady portrait,
and birds bring their lifetime
to the boughs.

Then even the corpse
light copies from below
may shimmer, dreaming it feels
the cheeks of blossom.

AT FIRST, AT LAST

At first the dips are shallow,
the peaks ever higher.
Until at last the peaks

are lower.
The valleys deepen.
It is a wave

that mounts and recoils.
Coming then to shadows
on the slopes,

rifts in the concaves,
what is there to do
but lie open-eyed and love

the wave? The wave that gave us
high joys
never again to be matched,

and shall give us,
till it breaks,
oh what

surprises, releases, abysses?
To feel! To feel!
To be the instrument

and the wound of feeling.
To lie open to feeling
on the exploding breast, the wave.

AT TRURO

The sea is unfolding scrolls
and rolling them up again.
It is an ancient diary

the waves are murmuring.
The words are white curls,
great capitals are seen

on the wrinkled swells.
Repeated rhythmically
it seems to me I read

my own biography.
Once I was a sea bird.
With beak a sharp pen,

I drew my signature on air.
There is a chapter when,
a crab, I slowly scratched

my name on a sandy page,
and once, a coral, wrote
a record of my age

on the wall of a water-grotto.
When I was a sea worm
I never saw the sun,

but flowed, a salty germ,
in the bloodstream of the sea.
There I left an alphabet

but it grew dim to me.
Something caught me in its net,
took me from the deep

book of the ocean, weaned me,
put fin and wing to sleep,
made me stand and made me

face the sun's dry eye.
On the shore of intellect
I forgot how to fly

above the wave, below it.
When my foot
touched land's thick back

it stuck like stem or root.
In brightness I lost track
of my underworld

of ultraviolet wisdom.
My fiery head furled
up its cool kingdom

and put night away.
The sea is unfolding scrolls,
and rolling them up.

As if the sun were blind
again I feel the suck
of the sea's dark mind.

. . . . 8 days without weighing anything.
Not knowing up from down.
Positioned for either breach birth
or urn burial. My mission the practice
of catching up by slowing down,
I am the culmination of a 10-storey bottle,
in 3 disconnectable parts,
being fueled with seething vapor
becoming water becoming fire.
I am the throbbing cork about to pop.

. . . . About to be dragged backward
through 121 sunsets,
not to bathe or drink bare light raw air.
My $75 pencil in my grotesque hand
prepares to float above the clipboard
strapped to my right knee.

. . . . T minus 10 and counting.
Over my obsolete epiderm redundant with
hairs and pits of moisture
I wear my new, rich, inflatable skin,
the bicep patch a proud tatoo,
a galaxy of 50 States,
my telemetric skull, a glossy cupola
resembling the glans of an Aztec god.
My sliding jaw, my safe transparent face
closes. Lungs, you will learn
to breathe hydrogen.

. . . . T minus 10 and counting.
Belted and bolted in, the capsule plugged,
when my 2 umbilical hoses tear free,
I shall increase to the bulk of 7 men,
be halfway to Africa in 12 minutes,
40 seconds. A bead beyond the bulge of earth,
extruded, banished. Till hooked to
the swivet of my ellipse,
I'm played through day and night and east
and west, reeled between apogee and perogee.

. . . . The erector stiffly swoons to its
concrete grave.

. . . . T minus 10 and holding.
Below in the blockhouse, pressed to the
neck of flame, a thumb on the piston
pulses LIFT OFF or ABORT.
My teleological aim the ovary moon,
will I ignite, jump, inject into the sky today
my sparkle of steel sperm?

. . . . Never so helpless, so choked with power.
Never so impotent, so important.
So naked, wrapped, equipped, and immobile,
cared for by 5000 nurses.
Let them siphon my urine to the nearest star.
Let it flare and spin like a Catherine.

. . . . T minus 10 . . . . The click of countdown stops.
My pram and mummycase, this trap's
tumescent tube's still locked to wet,
magnetic, unpredictable earth.
All my system's go, but oh,
an anger of the air won't let me go.
On the screen the blip is MISSION SCRUBBED.

. . . . Be dry my eye for nothing must leak
in here. If a tear forms, instruct the duct
to suck it back. Float, tadpole heart,
behind your slats of bone.
Keep your vibration steady, my switch of blood.
Eyeball in your nook of crepe
behind the ice-shield of my window-face,
and ear within your muff of radio,
count taps against the hatch's darkening pane.
Out on the dome some innocent drops of rain.
A puny jolt of thunder. Lightning's golden sneer.

A BASIN OF EGGS

Their cheeks touching,
their cheeks being
their bellies, their
bellies being undimpled,
dimples of dark being
blue chinks between
their touchings—
eggs in a basin in
a butcher's window

in strong sunlight
being elliptical
loops of primary whiteness.
In a pan their nudity
painful! Potential pain
of their being
damaged deranged de-arranged
against each others'
cheeks-and-bellies

or sides of the pan.
My like-curved eyeballs'
nooses chase their
smoothnesses
in the lattice-pattern's
blond and round design,
hunting clarities of being
yawed and yawned beyond
such birth-loops,

hinting at girths unpinched
by bruises of eclipse.
Sliced by blind rifts
between, my eyeballs
hurt from long looking
at the bone-looking
skin-thin bins
as yet uncracked,
and from yearning to exact

the fact of being
from white-bellied berries'
oblongs of light.
I feel how their cheeks
might grate like
bearings but for
buffers of my seeing
pads of shadow's bruise-
blue chinks between!

A BIRD'S LIFE

Is every day a separate life to a bird?
Else why,
as dawn finds the slit lid of starling- or sparrow-eye,
spurts that mad bouquet from agape bills?
Streamered, corkscrew, soprano tendrils
riot in the garden—
incredulous ejaculations at the first pinches
of birth— tiny winches
are tightened, then hysterically jerked loose.
There is produced
a bright geyser of metal-petaled sound
that, shredding, rubs its filings into my sleep.

As the sun, Herself, bulges from a crack in the cloud-shell,
a clamp is applied to every peep—
a paralysis of awe, at the ovening
under feathers of Mother Light—
a stun
of silence—then the reversion
to usual.

When the sun
is higher, only a blurt
of chitters, here and there,
from the sparrows—
sassy whistles, sarcastic barks from the starlings.
By noon they're into middle age
and the stodgy business of generation.

Evening, though, leaks
elegy from a few pathetic beaks.
Chirks of single-syllable despair

that the sky is empty and their
flit-lives almost done.
Their death is the death of light.
Do they lack memory, and so
not know
that The Hen
of the Sun
will hatch them again
next morning?

THE BLINDMAN

The blindman placed
a tulip on his tongue for purple's taste.
Cheek to grass, his green

was rough excitement's sheen
of little whips.
In water to his lips

he named the sea blue and white,
the basin of his tears and fallen beads of sight.
He said: This scarf is red;

I feel the vectors to its thread
that dance down from the sun. I know
the seven fragrances of the rainbow.

I have caressed
the orange hair of flames. Pressed
to my ear,

a pomegranate lets me hear
crimson's flute.
Trumpets tell me yellow. Only ebony is mute.

CARDINAL IDEOGRAMS

0   A mouth.   Can blow or breathe,
    be funnel, or Hello.

1   A grass blade or a cut.

2   A question seated.   And a proud
    bird's neck.

3   Shallow mitten for two-fingered hand.

4   Three-cornered hut
    on one stilt.   Sometimes built
    so the roof gapes.

5   A policeman.   Polite.
    Wearing visored cap.

6   O unrolling,
    tape of ambiguous length
    on which is written the mystery
    of everything curly.

7   A step,
    detached from its stair.

8   The universe in diagram:
    A cosmic hourglass.
    (Note enigmatic shape,
    absence of any valve of origin,
    how end overlaps beginning.)
    Unknotted like a shoelace
    and whipped back and forth,
    can serve as a model of time.

9   Lorgnette for the right eye.
    In England or if you are Alice
    the stem is on the left.

10 A grass blade or a cut
    companioned by a mouth.
    Open? Open. Shut? Shut.

CAUSE & EFFECT

Am *I* the bullet,
or the target,
or the hand
that holds the gun?
Or the whisper
in the brain saying *Aim, Fire?*
Is the bullet innocent though it kill?
Must the target stand unblinking and still?
Can one escape, the other stop, if it will?
Will the trigger-finger obey through force?
If the hand reverse command,
will the pregnant gun abort its curse?
The brain, the brain, surely *it* can refrain—
unclench the gun, break open
the pod of murder,
the target rise and run.
let the whisper must be caught,
But first the shot—
before the single wasp be burnt out,
the nest, infested, swarms with
before the multiple thought—
each sting the trigger pressed!

A CITY GARDEN IN APRIL

1 THE MAGNOLIA

In the shade
each tight cone

untwists to a goblet.
Under light

the rim widens,
splits like silk.
Seven spatulate

white flakes
float open, purple
dregs at the nape.

2 THE OLD AILANTHUS

Impossible to count
your fingers,

and all of them crooked.
How many tips

intending further tender
tips, in rigid grapple-

clusters weave with the
wind, with the shift

of the puffy rain cloud?
With the first big

honey-heat of the sun
you'll unloose

your secret explosion.
Then impossible to count

all the lubricious torches
in your labyrinth of arms.

3 DAFFODILS

Yellow telephones
in a row in the garden
are ringing,
shrill with light.

Old-fashioned spring
brings earliest models out
each April the same,
naïve and classical.

Look into the yolk-
colored mouthpieces
alert with echoes.
Say hello to time.

The sun's force
and the fountain's

cool hypnosis—
opposed purities

begin their marathon.
Colorless and motionful

the bowl feels twirl
a liquid hub,

the soft, incessant wheel
slurs over marble

until the dilation frays,
dribbling crystal strings.

The circle encircled,
the reborn circle

synchronized,
repeats the friction,

plash and whisper,
as of feathers rubbed

together or glossy hair.
Bounced from the sun's

breastplate, fierce colors
of flowers, fat leaves,

flinching birds—
while the gray dial

of water keeps all day
its constancy and flicker.

You've put out
new nooses since
yesterday.

With a hook and
a hook and a hook
you took territory

over brick,
seized that side
and knitted

outward to snare
the air with knots
and nipples of leaves.

Your old rope-root,
gray and dried,
made us think you'd

died self-strangled.
One day you inflated
a green parachute,

then breezily invented
a tent, and in five
you've proliferated

a whole plumed pavilion.
Not only alive
but splurging

up and out like a geyser.
Old Faithful,
it's worth a winter

hung up stiff
in sullen petrifaction
for such excess.

COLORS WITHOUT OBJECTS

Colors without objects—colors alone—
wriggle in the tray of my eye,

incubated under the great flat lamp
of the sun:

bodiless blue, little razor-streak,
yellow melting like a firework petal,

double purple yo-yo
in a broth of murky gold.

Sharp green squints I have never seen
minnow-dive the instant they're alive;

bulb-reds with flickering cilia
dilate, but then implode

to discs of impish scotomata
that flee into the void;

weird orange slats of hot thought
about to make a basket—but

there is no material here—they slim
to a snow of needles, are erased.

Now a mottling takes place.
All colors fix chromosomic links

that dexterously mix,
flip, exchange their aerial ladders.

Such stunts of speed and metamorphosis
breed impermanent, objectless acts,

a thick, a brilliant bacteria—
but most do not survive.

I wait for a few iridium specks of idea
to thrive in the culture of my eye.

DEAR ELIZABETH *

Yes, I'd like a pair of *Bicos de Lacre*—
meaning beaks of "lacquer" or "sealing wax"?
(the words are the same in Portuguese)
". . . about 3 inches long including the tail,
red bills and narrow bright red masks . . ."
You say the male has a sort of "drooping
mandarin-mustache—one black stripe"—

otherwise the sexes are alike. "Tiny but
plump, shading from brown and gray on top
to pale beige, white, and a rose red spot
on the belly"—their feathers, you tell
me, incredibly beautiful "alternating
lights and darks like nearly invisible
wave-marks on a sandflat at low tide,

and with a pattern so fine one must put on
reading glasses to appreciate it properly."
Well, do they sing? If so, I expect their
note is extreme. Not something one hears,
but must watch the cat's ears to detect.
And their nest, that's "smaller than a fist,
with a doorway in the side just wide enough

for each to get into to sleep." They must
be very delicate, not easy to keep. Still,
on the back porch on Perry St., here, I'd
build them a little Brazil. I'd save every
shred and splinter of New York sunshine
and work through the winter to weave them
a bed. A double, exactly their size,

* A reply to Elizabeth Bishop in Brazil.

with a roof like the Ark. I'd make sure to
leave an entrance in the side. I'd set it
in among the morning-glories where the
gold-headed flies, small as needles' eyes,
are plentiful. Although "their egg is apt
to be barely as big as a baked bean . . ."
It rarely hatches in captivity, you mean—

but we could hope! In today's letter you
write, "The *Bicos de Lacre* are adorable as
ever—so tiny, neat, and taking baths
constantly in this heat, in about ¼ inch
of water—then returning to their *filthy*
little nest to lay another egg—which
never hatches." But here it might! And it

doesn't matter that "their voice is weak,
they have no song." I can see them as I
write—on their perch on my porch. "From
the front they look like a pair of half-
ripe strawberries"—except for that stripe.
"At night the cage looks empty" just as
you say. I have "a moment's fright"—

then see the straw nest moving softly.
Yes, dear Elizabeth, if you would be so
kind, I'd like a pair of *Bicos de Lacre*—
especially as in your P.S. you confess,
"I already have two unwed female wild
canaries, for which I must find husbands
in order to have a little song around here."

DRAWING THE CAT

Makes a platform for himself:
forepaws bent under his chest,
slot-eyes shut in a corniced head,
haunches high like a wing chair,
hindlegs parallel, a sled.

As if on water, low afloat
like a wooden duck: a bundle not
apt to be tipped, so symmetrized
on hidden keel of tail he rides
squat, arrested, glazed.

Lying flat, a violin:
hips are splayed, head and chin
sunk on paws, stem straight out
from the arched root
at the clef-curve of the thighs.

Wakes: the head ball rises.
Claws sprawl. Wires
go taut, make a wicket of his spine.
He humps erect, with scimitar yawn
of hooks and needles porcupine.

Sits, solid as a doorstop,
tail-encircled, tip laid on his toes,
ear-tabs stiff, gooseberry eyes
full, unblinking, sourly wise.
In outline: a demijohn with a pewter look.

Swivels, bends a muscled neck:
petal-of-tulip-tongue slicks

the brushpoint of his tail to black,
then smooths each glossy epaulette
with assiduous sponge.

Whistle him into a canter
into the kitchen: tail hooked aside,
ears at the ready. Elegant copy
of carrousel pony—
eyes bright as money.

11TH FLOOR, WEST 4TH STREET

From a little window high in a shaft
I look at many-windowed giant crates,
lit factories jumbled in the loft
of beginning night. Sluggish coils of
sundown low on the wall of sky
behind the river—its glimmer moves,
a stamp-sized square of prickled waves
between tall rulers of the western street.
Blue-white light in the shells of the
crates that bulk their corners on the valley
of beginning night; light-riddled the trough
of the southern street where trinket-vehicles
double-trickle to the anvil-end of Manhattan,

toward the squat trunks of towers;
their jutting tops curved or coned,
crossed with wires of windowed light,
lift stiff and slender into the high apse
of night. In space, at level of my eye,
the early dark is clean of objects,
except three: the new emphatic moon
a comma of light, and two flies of light
that wigwag red and green, crawling a pane
of slate into the east.
                                    The ruddy smudge
has darkened on the wall now, low by the river.
Copper-green, the drape of maturing night
rides down in loops of shadow to the street.
I see along its edges slow dolls,
dressed in thickening cloth of dark,

pushing their shades like barrows as they walk
beneath the trinket-lamps. And all the upright
radiant walls, the jagged lighted gorge
of the southern street, is theirs—
their scene, their stage, their making—
soft innocuous puppets there below
wobbling on the sidewalks of their show.

FABLE FOR WHEN THERE'S NO WAY OUT

Grown too big for his skin,
and it grown hard,

without a sea and atmosphere—
he's drunk it all up—

his strength's inside him now,
but there's no room to stretch.

He pecks at the top
but his beak's too soft;

though instinct and ambition shoves,
he can't get through.

Barely old enough to bleed
and already bruised!

In a case this tough
what's the use

if you break your head
instead of the lid?

Despair tempts him
to just go limp:

Maybe the cell's
already a tomb,

and beginning end
in this round room.

Still, stupidly he pecks
and pecks, as if from under

his own skull—
yet makes no crack . . .

No crack until
he finally cracks,

and kicks and stomps.
What a thrill

and shock to feel
his little gaff poke

through the floor!
A way he hadn't known or meant.

Rage works if reason won't.
When locked up, bear down.

FLAG OF SUMMER

Sky and sea and sand,
fabric of the day.
The eye compares each band.

Parallels of color on bare
canvas of time-by-the-sea.
Linen-clean the air.

Tan of the burlap
beach scuffed with prints
of bathers. Green and dapple,

the serpentine swipe
of the sea unraveling
a ragged crepe

on the shore. Heavy satin
far out, the coil,
darkening, flattens

to the sky's rim.
There a gauze screen,
saturate-blue, shimmers.

Blue and green and tan,
the fabric changes hues
by brush of light or rain:

sky's violet bar
leans over flinty waves
opaque as the shore's

opaline grains; sea silvers,
clouds fade to platinum,
the sand-mat ripples

with greenish tints
of snakeskin, or drying,
whitens to tent-cloth

spread in the sun. These bands,
primary in their dimensions,
elements, textures, strands:

the flag of summer,
emblem of ease, triple-striped,
each day salutes the swimmer.

FLYING HOME FROM UTAH

Forests are branches of a tree lying down,
its blurred trunk in the north.
Farms are fitted pieces of a floor,

tan and green tiles that get smoother,
smaller, the higher we fly.
Heel-shaped dents of water I know are deep

from here appear opaque, of bluish glass.
Curl after curl, rivers are coarse locks
unravelling southward over the land;

hills, rubbed felt, crumpled bumps
of antlers pricking from young buck's heads.
Now towns are scratches here and there

on a wide, brown-bristled hide.
Long roads rayed out from the sores of cities
begin to fester and crawl with light—

above them the plane is a passing insect
that eyes down there remark, forget
in the moment it specks the overcast.

It climbs higher. Clouds become ground.
Pillows of snow meet, weld into ice.
Alone on a moonlit stainless rink

glides the ghost of a larva, the shadow
of our plane. Lights go on
in the worm-belly where we sit;

it becomes the world, and seems to cease
to travel—only vibrates, stretched out tense
in the tank of night.

The room of my mind replaces the long, lit room.
I dream I point my eye over a leaf
and fascinate my gaze upon its veins:

A sprawled leaf, many-fingered, its radial
ridges limber, green—but curled,
tattered, pocked, the brown palm

nibbled by insects, nestled in by worms:
One leaf of a tree that's one tree of a forest,
that's the branch of the vein of a leaf

of a tree. Perpetual worlds
within, upon, above the world, the world
a leaf within a wilderness of worlds.

FOUR-WORD LINES

Your eyes are just
like bees, and I
feel like a flower.
Their brown power makes
a breeze go over
my skin. When your
lashes ride down and
rise like brown bees'
legs, your pronged gaze
makes my eyes gauze.
I wish we were
in some shade and
no swarm of other
eyes to know that
I'm a flower breathing
bare, laid open to
your bees' warm stare.
I'd let you wade
in me and seize
with your eager brown
bees' power a sweet
glistening at my core.

GODS | CHILDREN

They are born naked
And without tails
They cannot fly
Their blood is red
They are children until they die
And then "are God's children"
Are gods . . . children . . .
Are *gods children?*

Worlds are their heads
Oceans infants' serene eyes
Blue and green they invented
Leaves did not grow
or the wind blow
until their spine
lifted like a tendril
Their tongue curled
Their hand made a sign

They are not like fruit
though their skin is sweet
Though they rot they have wrought
the numbers one to ten
They founded the sun
When the sun found them
it undertook its path and aim
The moon also
when it received its name
The air first heard itself called glory
in their lungs

Beasts they placed in the sky
and in their caves
and on their platforms
For they remembered their cradles

Their blood in flow
told them their beginnings
The beloved hooves
massy necks
rich nostrils
sex a red coal in the groin
they worshipped
Also their helical rod
called evil and sapience

They sorcelled angels
dreamed queerer forms
On the brain's map fixed a junction INFINITY
In the entrails' maze PROPHECY
And made MEASURE
And the dance of the PARTICLES
With a switch the system TIME turned on
A braided chain
torque for the whole of space
their game

They play
are flexible jugglers and jongleurs
fashioners of masks
Are mirror-makers
and so dupe themselves
Dress themselves
are terrified at flesh
Think each other phantoms
idols
demons
toys
Make of each other handles
ladders
quicksands
Are to each other houses of safety
hammocks of delight

They cannot fly
But nest themselves in bullets
In there dressed as embryos
they shoot themselves in a circle
out beyond their ball
And can breathe with such a placenta
their foot floating
far separate from its ground

Before
in iron capsules lived under the sea
in baskets inflated rode the air
Many other marvels built besides
Are mysterious charts
beneath their skulls' membranes
And have invented madness

Under their bodies' casings
in intricate factories
work their strong soft engines
Their blood is red
Color and name they invented
and so created it
And have named themselves

And it is even so
that they operate upon one another
and increase
and make replicas
and replace one another
new for old
and tick to death
like moments

When they are dead
they are made naked
Are washed and dressed
They do this for each other
like children
And are fixed into fine boxes
like children fix their dolls

And then?
"Are God's children"
Are gods . . . children . . .
Then are gods children?

HEARING THE WIND AT NIGHT

I heard the wind coming,
transferred from tree to tree.
I heard the leaves
swish, wishing to be free

to come with the wind, yet wanting to stay
with the boughs like sleeves.
The wind was a green ghost.
Possessed of tearing breath

the body of each tree
whined, a whipping post,
then straightened and resumed
its vegetable oath.

I heard the wind going,
and it went wild.
Somewhere the forest threw itself
into tantrum like a child.

I heard the trees tossing
in punishment or grief,
then sighing, and soughing,
soothing themselves to sleep.

HIS SUICIDE

He looked down at his withering body and saw a hair
near his navel, swaying.

And now he saw his other hairs rise up.

He felt a hectic current in his veins.
Looking within, he saw the bubbling of his blood.

He cursed his fever, saying:
"It is the chemistry of prayer.
It increases in frequency,
seeding panic to all my being.
My cells swell with the liquid of guilt they fabricate,
juices of hatred eat my belly
my corpuscles make war in me as they devour each other.
My head heats in the combustion of anxiety,
I am polluted by the secretions of my soul's decay,
while my brain wears away
with the scratching night and day
on the encephalograph of prayer.
I grow monstrous with the leukemia of the world."

And he heard the hair say: "Hear me."
And he saw it grow gray as it waved.
All his hairs he saw whiten,
and, numberless, wilt from their erect electric listening.
He saw them topple from their roots.
"How dare you!" he cursed them.
There surged a brief resuscitation to his body.
His heart took heart and pounded twice
with the health of fear
But then the plague of prayer redoubled and overwhelmed him.

In his feebleness he raged, and said:
"I will tear out this evil and free it."

With his withered hands he tore the remaining hairs
from his body and head.
With his nails he opened his breast,
and with his fist he exploded his heart,
which erupted, a black and red volcano.

As his brain tasted, for the first time,
the birth of his doom,
he became a rolling tide, a floating mountain of ecstasy.
"I see you! I love you!" his eyes cried,
overflowing with his bright blood.
"You were the light of the world
that are now my gushing tears—
the kind and fiery tears of chaos, that wash my eyes
with the cure of oblivion."

"He hears us!" cried his sick blood
pouring from his ears.
"Even as of old he heard our hair before it perished."

With his last strength, the chemistry of prayer,
a few drops of his blood coagulated.
That clot whirled out, free, in the vortex of the universe.

IN A MUSEUM CABINET

Like some kind of ruin, but domed
like an igloo . . . Midway in the mound
are two deep punctures of darkness
more square than round—thick-walled
"casements," those transparencies

that filtered light lost long ago.
Where the nose was, a rough diamond-shape
positioned on the sill of the lip-ridge . . .
I can see, as through a "front door"
agape, thin steps of debris within.

Heavy, squat, like a blockhouse,
but bombed out . . . This makes it look frail.
The card says: *Unearthed in London.*
Roman. 100 A.D. It could also be
some wild den, scoured by a hurricane,

its stones so stubborn they settled
into fissures where the cheekbones hinge,
did not quite crumble. Or, again,
it could be the beast of that den
petrified to rock. It crouches

on side-teeth still strong. The wide
underjaw is gone. The forehead
is whole, smooth, and round. But an old
fracture slants from the left socket
to a tooth-root, like a trench for tears.

It crouches, gripping the glass ground
with teeth and the blunt points of the
neck-pocket. Looking at it, I hear
an eerie wind whirl in and out,
as through gray caves of coral by the sea.

IN THE HAIR OF THE NIGHT

The hound's eye of the sun
and the cat's eye of the moon
watch the earth's eye,
the iris of a mouse,
in the cloudy hair of the night.

The sun's eye sees
In the hair of the night
the cloudy head of a sphinx
whose face is a herd of eyes
in the monstrous hair of the night.

The moon's eye sees a snake,
in the cloudy mouth of the night,
that uncoils, uncovers the nine
diamonds of its eyes
in the monstrous face of a sphinx.

The earth's eye is the iris of a mouse
in the cloudy mouth of a snake
in the face of a sphinx
whose head is a herd of monstrous eyes
in the hair of the night.

THE KITE

Triangular face, or mask,
dangling a spinal cord,

or like the diagram of a spirochete,
the tail wiggling.

Desperate paper pollywog, aloft,
pushing upstream,

alive because wind pours over, under
it, like water.

The sky with invisible wind,
the frame of Being around a face,

behind the unprobed surface
the mirror's space.

"Perhaps all things are inanimate
and it is the void that lives,"

I think, until I remember
that a string,

not seen in the white air,
is tied to a finger below.

The paper face is fixed
in a magnetic flow

on which it depends,
by which it is repelled.

The tug of the void,
the will of the world

together declare
placement for the shivering mask.

THE LIGHTNING

The lightning waked me. It slid unde r
my eyelid. A black book flipped ope n
to an illuminated page. Then insta ntly
shut. Words of destiny were being ut-
tered in the distance. If only I could
make them out. . . . Next day as I lay
in the sun, a symbol for concei ving the
universe was scratched on my e yeball.
But quickly its point eclipse d, and
softened, in the scabbard of my brain.

My cat speaks one word. F our vowels
and a consonant. He rece ives with the
hairs of his body the wh ispers of the
stars. The kinglet spe aks by flashing
into view a ruby feath er on his head.
He is held by a threa d to the eye of the
sun, and cannot fall into error. Any
flower is a perfect ear. Or else it is
a thousand lips. . . . When will I grope my
way clear of the entrails of intellect?

THE LITTLE RAPIDS

Over its cliff
splashes the
little rapids,
a braid of glossy
motion in perpetual
flow and toss,
its current rayed
flashing down
crayon veins.

Life-node of my
precipice of bone,
a snake-mouth muscle
spills urgent venom
to soft hills,
to flesh-warm stone.

A replica of all
power's crotched
here in the ribs,
knot and nubbin
of the jutting flood.
Leaps and drops
are instants in
the swirling hour
reiterated from
this hub:

Grief-gusher,
freshet of desire,
snug nest of joy
and fear,
its zest constant
even in sleep,
its padded roar
bounding in the
grotto of the breast.

Hinge of hate and
love, steep springhead,
riddle of my blood,
primal pool of
cruelty, and all
queer sweet thrills . . .
Ravine of my body,
red, incredulous
with autumn,
from here curt death
will hurl me delirious
into the gorge.

MORE RICH

When I go blind I shall see
my dreams

that round the edges of my mind
flash sometimes

then sink in the inverted sea.
Each thing the sun

makes hard and my hand takes
shall dissolve

a pure void underhemisphere
reveal its pole

When tensions of the light
relax there'll be

a waveless plunge. I'll cast
my shape

and weight and have no hinge
and have no

mental hook. Blind I'll dive
and read

the colored flood.
A world

more rich than blood shall be
my book.

MOTHERHOOD

She sat on a shelf,
her breasts two bellies
on her poked-out belly,
on which the navel looked
like a sucked-in mouth—
her knees bent and apart,
her long left arm raised,
with the large hand knuckled
to a bar in the ceiling—
her right hand clamping
the skinny infant to her chest—
its round, pale, new,
soft muzzle hunting
in the brown hair for a nipple,
its splayed, tiny hand picking
at her naked, dirty ear.
Twisting its little neck,
with tortured, ecstatic eyes
the size of lentils, it looked
into her severe, close-set,
solemn eyes, that beneath bald
eyelids glared— dull lights
in sockets of leather.

She twitched some chin-hairs,
with pain or pleasure,
as the baby-mouth found and
yanked at her nipple;
its pink-nailed, jointless
fingers, wandering her face,
tangled in the tufts

of her cliffy brows.
She brought her big
hand down from the bar—
with pretended exasperation
unfastened the little hand,
and locked it within her palm—
while her right hand,
with snag-nailed forefinger
and short, sharp thumb, raked
the new orange hair
of the infant's skinny flank—
and found a louse,
which she lipped, and
thoughtfully crisped
between broad teeth.
She wrinkled appreciative
nostrils which, without a nose,
stood open— damp, holes
above the poke of her mouth.

She licked her lips, flicked
her leather eyelids—
then, suddenly flung
up both arms and grabbed
the bars overhead.
The baby's scrabbly fingers
instantly caught the hair—
as if there were metal rings there—
in her long, stretched armpits.
And, as she stately swung,
and then proudly, more swiftly
slung herself from corner
to corner of her cell—

arms longer than her round
body, short knees bent—
her little wild-haired,
poke-mouthed infant hung,
like some sort of trophy,
or decoration, or shaggy medal—
shaped like herself— but new,
clean, soft and shining
on her chest.

NAKED IN BORNEO

(From a painting by Tobias)

They wear air
or water like a skin,
their skin the smoothest suit.
Are tight and loose
as the leopard, or sudden
and still as the moccasin.
Their blouse is black

shadows of fronds
on a copper vest of sun.
Glossy rapids are
their teeth and eyes
beneath straight harsh blonds
of rained-on grain that thatch
their round head-huts.

Long thongs their bodies, bows
or canoes. Both tense and lax
their bodies, spears
they tool, caress, hoard, decorate
with cuts. Their fears
are their weapons. Coiled or
straight they run up trees

and on jungle thorns; their feet
are their shoes, fiercehair
their hats that hold off sun's hate.
They glide, muscles of water
through water, dark oil-beads
pave their lashing
torsos. Are bare in air,

are wind-combed, armpit and groin;
are taut arrows turned sinuous reeds
for dancing on drumskin ground.
Rasped by the sun's tongue, then moon-licked
all their slick
moist feathered shafts
in the hammocks of tangled thighs

the silks of night plash among.
Their joys, their toys are their children
who as kittens ride
their mother's neck, or wrestle
with the twins of her breasts
where she squats by the meal pot.
At hunter's naked side

little hunter stalks fix-eyed,
miniature poison-dart
lifted, learning the game:
young pointer in the bush,
fish-diver in the river,
grave apprentice in the art
of magic pain

when the blood pines
to be let a little,
to sharpen the friction of Alive,
in the feckless skin
leave some slits and signs
that old spirit leaked out,
new spirit sneaked in.

OCEAN WHALE-SHAPED

Ocean, whale-shaped, rocking between the dunes,
in the gateway of their great naked knees,
horizon chafing a tame sky,

your vast back purple, your shoreward side
wallowing blue, fretted with racing foam,
green, then diamond your fin flashes on sand.

Glazed monuments of the wind, the dunes,
their sprawling limbs Olympian lift and fall
to slopes and platforms seeming hard as bone,

but footsteps scar their flanks like snow;
their white bodies shift,
are shunted by you, blue-black boisterous whale—

and whittled, are rewhittled by the wind
unsatisfied with any shape or perpetuity.
The land, the sand we tread is not the steady

element our feet believe.
Indelible ocean humped beside the sky,
you unsubstantial we can't grasp or walk on,

you pry at these gates and break them when you will—
Overwhelming whale of water, mover and shaper,
over and over carving your cradle here.

OCTOBER TEXTURES

The brushy and hairy,
tassely and slippery

willow, fragmitie,
cattail, goldenrod.

The fluttery, whistley
water-dimpling divers,

waders, shovelers,
coots and rocking scaup.

Big blue, little green,
horned grebe, godwit,

bufflehead, ruddy,
marsh hawk, clapper rail.

Striated water
and striated feather.

The breast of the sunset.
The phalarope's breast.

OF ROUNDS

MOON
      round
          goes around while going around a
                              round
                                EARTH.
EARTH
      round
          with MOON
                  round
                  going around while going around,
goes around while going around a
                    round
                      SUN.
SUN
    round
        with EARTH
              round
               with MOON
                    round
                        going around while going
around, and MERCURY
                round
              and VENUS
                  round
                    going around while
going around, and MARS
                round
               with two MOONS
                      round
                      round
                        going around
while going around, and JUPITER
                  round
                with twelve MOONS
                          round
                          round
                          round
                          round
                          round
                          round
                          round
                          round
                          round
                          round
                          round
                          round
                          round

74

going around while going around, and SATURN
                                        round
                                              with nine

MOONS
          round
          round
          round
          round
          round
          round
          round
          round
          round
              going around while going around, and URANUS
                                                        round

with five MOONS
                  round
                  round
                  round
                  round
                  round
                    going around while going around, and NEPTUNE
round
      with two MOONS
                      round
                      round
                          going around while going around, and

PLUTO
        round
              going around while going around, goes around while
going around
              A   OF ROUNDS
                                              Round

                                                              75

ON HANDLING SOME SMALL SHELLS
FROM THE WINDWARD ISLANDS*

Their scrape and clink
together of musical coin.

       Than the tinkling of crickets
       more eerie, more thin.

Their click as of crystal,
wood, carapace and bone.

       A tintinabular fusion.
       Their friction spinal and chill

as of ivory embryo
fragments of horn

       honed to whistles and flutes.
       Windy Eustachian coils

cold as the sea till held,
then warm as the palm,

       and snuggled naturally there
       smoother than skin.

The curve and continuous
spiral intrinsic, their

       role eternal inversion,
       the closed, undulant scroll.

* A gift from N.B. and D.E.

Even when corrugate,
sharpness rubbed from

　　　　　　their forms, licked by
　　　　　　the mouth of the sea

to tactile charms.
Some blanched by the eye

　　　　　　of the sun, a pumice shine
　　　　　　buffing their calcareous

nakedness clean as a tooth.
Some colored like flesh,

　　　　　　but more subtle than
　　　　　　corpuscle dyes. Some

sunsets, some buttermilk
skies, or penumbras

　　　　　　of moons in eclipse.
　　　　　　Malachite greens, fish-eyed

icy blues, pigeon-foot pinks,
brindled fulvous browns,

　　　　　　but most white like tektites.
　　　　　　Gathered here in a bowl,

their ineradicable inks
vivid, declarative

under water. Peculiar fossil-
fruits that suck through ribbed

lips and gaping sutures
into secret clefts

the sweet wet with a tame taste.
Vulviform creatures, or

rather their rocklike
backs with labial bellies.

Some earhole shaped, or
funnels with an overlap,

some stony worms curled up
and glazed, the egress

like a trumpet. Some cones
with tight twisted sphincters

rugos and spiculate,
cactus-humped or warted,

others slick and simple
pods where tender jellies hid.

The frigid souls, the
amorphous ones, emptied

from out their skeletons
that were their furled caves.

78

Each an eccentric
mummy-case, one facet mute

        and ultimate, one baffling
        in its ruffles as a rose.

The largest, a valve of
bone streaked like a cloud,

        its shadowy crease a pinched
        ambiguous vestibule, a puckered

trap ajar. The sly inviting
smile into the labyrinth.

ON SEEING ROCKS CROPPING OUT
OF A HILL IN CENTRAL PARK

Boisterous water arrested, these rocks
are water's body in death. Transparent

water falling without stop makes a wall,
the frenzied soul of rock its white breath.

Dark water's inflated wave, harsh spray
is ghost of a boulder and cave's

marble, agitated drapery. Stillness
water screams for, flying forth,

the body of death. Rock dreams
soul's motion, its hard birth.

OUT OF THE SEA, EARLY

A bloody
egg yolk. A burnt hole
spreading in a sheet. An en-
raged rose threatening to bloom.
A furnace hatchway opening, roaring.
A globular bladder filling with immense
juice. I start to scream. A red hydrocepha-
lic head is born, teetering on the stump of
its neck. When it separates, it leaks rasp-
berry from the horizon down the wide esca-
lator. The cold blue boiling waves cannot
scour out that band, that broadens, sliding toward me up the wet sand slope.
The fox-hair grows, grows thicker
on the upfloating head. By
six o'clock, diffused to
ordinary gold,
it exposes each silk thread and rumple in the carpet.

THE PEOPLE WALL*

Prodded by the smiles of handsome clerks,
they file into the narrow slits, and are filed,
500 every 20 minutes on 12 variecolored shelves.
All are carefully counted; all but their names are known.

It's been shown that 50 hips from the Midwest,
mainly female, with a random sprinkling of male and
juvenile, can fit into any given row, elbow to elbow
along the rail, heels hooked under the padded

8-inch-wide seat bar. Now the steep drawer
is filled, all the heads are filed, the racks closed
by the clerks at the ends of each aisle.
"Hello there!" calls the sartorially perfect head

clerk, let down on a circular podium to stand as if
in the air. He's propped like a stopped pendulum
in front of the wall of people all filed and smiling.
It's a colorful assortment of United States faces, good-

looking for the most part, fun-ready, circus-
expectant, and bright as a box of glazed marzipan.
"Hello there, all you people!" Twirling his
microphone cable like a lariat: "Do you know

where you're going on this Fair day? You're
going to be lifted . . . by mighty hydraulic arms . . .
straight up . . . 90 feet . . . up into The Egg!
In there you're going to learn how your mind works . . .

* At the IBM pavilion, New York World's Fair, 1965.

in color . . . on 15 separate screens . . . a show
that will show you how you all think! What do you think
of that? Now, just relax. Lean back. And no
smoking, please. Everybody comfortable? No need

to hold on to anything. Don't hold on to your hats,
or even your heads. Just lean back and get ready
for a pleasant ride backwards . . . There you go!
Up . . . up . . . up into the World of the Computers!"

Down on the ground, thousands of identical plastic
balls cascade through the maze of The Probability
Machine, repeatedly testing the Theory of the
Frequency of Errors. Clicking musically, they choose

their individual ways down, bouncing once before they
settle into the common heap. Each ball might
land in any one of 21 chutes, yet each chute fills
to about the same height each time the balls descend.

The magic curve completes itself. All balls
have fallen, and form a more or less symmetrical
black hill. A cheerful bell trills. The People Wall
rises. All heads, filed and smiling, are fed into The Egg.

THE PREGNANT DREAM

I had a dream in which I had a dream,
and in my dream I told you, "Listen,
I will tell you my dream." And I
began to tell you. And you told me,
"I haven't time to listen while you
tell your dream."

Then in my dream I dreamed I began to
forget my dream. And I forgot my dream.
And I began to tell you, "Listen, I
have forgot my dream." And now I tell
you: "Listen while I tell you my dream,
a dream in which I dreamed I forgot
my dream," and I begin to tell you:
"In my dream you told me, 'I haven't
time to listen.' "

And you tell me: "You dreamed I wouldn't
listen to a dream that you forgot?
I haven't time to listen to forgotten
dreams." "But I haven't forgot I
dreamed," I tell you, "a dream in which
I told you, 'Listen, I have forgot,'
and you told me, 'I haven't time.' "
"I haven't time," you tell me.

And now I begin to forget that I forgot
what I began to tell you in my dream.
And I tell you, "Listen, listen, I
begin to forget."

RAIN AT WILDWOOD

The rain fell like grass growing
upside down in the dark,
at first thin shoots,
short, crisp, far apart,

but, roots in the clouds,
a thick mat grew
quick, loquacious, lachrymose blades
blunt on the tent top.

The grass beneath ticked,
trickled, tickled like rain
all night, inchwormed
under our ears,

its flat liquid tips slipping
east with the slope.
Various tin plates
and cups and a bucket filled

up outside,
played, plinked, plicked,
plopped till guttural.
The raccoon's prowl was almost

silent in the trash,
soggy everything but eggshells.
No owl called.
Waking at first light

the birds were blurred,
notes and dyes of jay and towhee
guaranteed to bleed.
And no bluing in the sky.

In the inverted V
of the tent flaps
muddy sheets of morning
slumped among the trunks,

but the pin oaks' veridian
dripping raggedy leaves
on the wood's floor released
tangy dews and ozones.

THE SECRET IN THE CAT

I took my cat apart
to see what made him purr.
Like an electric clock
or like the snore

of a warming kettle,
something fizzed and sizzled in him.
Was he a soft car,
the engine bubbling sound?

Was there a wire beneath his fur,
or humming throttle?
I undid his throat.
Within was no stir.

I opened up his chest
as though it were a door:
no whisk or rattle there.
I lifted off his skull:

no hiss or murmur.
I halved his little belly
but found no gear,
no cause for static.

So I replaced his lid,
laced his little gut.
His heart into his vest I slid
and buttoned up his throat.

His tail rose to a rod
and beckoned to the air.
Some voltage made him vibrate
warmer than before.

Whiskers and a tail:
perhaps they caught
some radar code
emitted as a pip, a dot-and-dash

of woolen sound.
My cat a kind of tuning fork?—
amplifier?—telegraph?—
doing secret signal work?

His eyes elliptic tubes:
there's a message in his stare.
I stroke him
but cannot find the dial.

SIGHTSEEING IN PROVINCETOWN

If your elbow were   an eagle's head
and your loins   the mouth of a cat
its tongue   many ripped tongues of flame

and if your ribs were   the membranous wings of a dragon
and if one leg   were of black leather
the bloody claw of a chicken   grafted to the knee

and if your buttocks were   the cheeks of a laughing insane face
the lips clasping   a trumpet
from which wasps were flying   the wasps' eyes clearly seen

glossy with mad hilarity   and if although you were male
your left breast were   a large pale polyp
with numerous nipples   and the other breast a dog's head

its jaws straining   to swallow a severed thigh
and if from your slick head   that of a rhinoceros
with inrolled eyes   there curved instead of a snout

a snake   with a fishhook through its neck
and if rags of flame   flew from your navel
it being the unhinged door   of a furnace

and if   looking down
you saw a cat's mouth   between your legs
giving birth   to the dripping lower half

of a face whose skin peeled back   hung from the earlobes
with raw lips stretched   in a sonorous scream
and if in the gullet's vortex   there bobbed

a tiny figure scalded red   a Janus-faced child
both girl and boy   impaled through one armpit
by a tooth   then you'd be elected

Chief Lucifer   of S. H. Masters' Hell
the colors like flesh   like silk like fruit
under an exceptionally clear patina   smooth as petunia

"The Last Judgment"   (Austria c. 1480)
gilt-framed   on a plum-velvet-covered wall
in Provincetown   1965

SLEEPING OVERNIGHT ON THE SHORE

Earth turns
        one cheek to the sun
while the other tips
        its crags and dimples into shadow.
We say sun comes up,
        goes down,
but it is our planet's incline
        on its shy invisible neck.
The smooth skin of the sea,
        the bearded buttes of the land
blush orange,
        we say it is day.
Then earth in its turning
        slips half of itself away
from the ever burning.
        Night's frown
smirches earth's face,
        by those hours marked older.
It is dark, we say.
        But night is a fiction
hollowed at the back of our ball,
        when from its obverse side
a cone of self-thrown shade
        evades the shining,
and black and gray
        the cinema of dreams streams through
our sandgrain skulls
        lit by our moon's outlining.

Intermittent moon
          that we say climbs
or sets, circles only.
               Earth flicks it past its shoulder.
It tugs at the teats of the sea.
          And sky
is neither high
          nor is earth low.
There is no dark
          but distance
between stars.
          No dawn,
for it is always day
          on Gas Mountain, on the sun—
and horizon's edge
          the frame of our eye.

Cool sand on which we lie
          and watch the gray waves
clasp, unclasp
          a restless froth of light,
silver saliva of the sucking moon—
          whose sun is earth
who's moon to the sun—
          To think this shore,
each lit grain plain
          in the foot-shaped concaves
heeled with shadow,
          is pock or pocket
on an aging pin
          that juggler sun once threw,

made twirl among
        those other blazing objects out
around its crown.
        And from that single toss
the Nine still tumble—
        swung in a carousel of staring light,
where each rides ringleted
        by its pebble-moons—
white lumps of light
        that are never to alight,
for there is no down.

SPECTRUM ANALYSIS

When I say
    I
    I swim
in a yellow
    room.
When I think
    my mind
    my mind
pulls to me a
    sun
that magnetizes to itself a
    million
    million
butterflies dandelions and
coins eggyolks strands
of ambergris the eyes
of cats and owls and
beakers ampouls beads
of topaz and of honey and of
    urine.

Have I arrived from
    left or
    right to hover here
in the clear permission of my
    temperature? Is my
    flow a fading
    up or
    down—my glow
    going? Or is my flush
    rushing to a rose of ripe
    explosion?

Outside the wall
        I call
        east the scene is
        green
        I name
        naming *my*
        name. And
        west beyond this
    room looms brazen in heathaze
of imagination an
        orange doom
if my destiny's so spelled.

Saying
        I feel
        I feel
        I flicker out toward cooler
        cells through
        green down
        blue to darkening
        indigo wells.
If these are
        downhills and not
        upslants I'm engulfed
in the throat of a vast
        petunia unknown
        to bone or
        moon.

In that atmosphere immeasurably rare—
and is it
      high or
      deep?—
have I already been iced an
      ultraviolet inkling
in my narrowest
      sleep? Perhaps
      unless the pass is
      counterwise and
      I whirl—not
      grassward but
      brassward
rammed with the rusty
      dust through spirals of
      radiation
crammed flaked corroded dispersed
      particulated
to electron
      pits my
      I dissected
      naked
frayed to anonymous
      its—reversed and
      tossed out
      lost—so
      around in the
      boundless loosed.

Yet while
      I say
      I
      I swim

defined in a
> yellow
> room. Though
> I know not what
> point *my*
> *point*
> points to
> it is a
> point intent upon
> itself and in
> its speed so steady bent
> it seems entirely still.
> Pointing
> its
> *it* to
> itself
> it's spent

upon its journey
the jagged jig around the centrifuge.

Until
> I say
> *I*
> *will*
> will
> I be distilled in the
> red
> room there next
> door within the
> core of an
> orbital rose that

decaying to
its bud will freeze to
its seed?
Yes
I say
yes and consent to
less and
less.

Unless
the race is to unfurling where
lips within
lips proliferate
their lace outleaping all edges
to compel gigantic
bloom. Then
blood again? *My*
blood beneath my skin?

When I taste
I
I taste something akin
to suprafruit or neutronic
flower
a solar heart engorged with light's rich
juice
infrared.

STILL TURNING

Under a round roof the flying
horses, held by their heels to the disk of the
floor, move to spurts from a pillar of
    music, cranked from the past like grainy

honey. Their ears are wood, their nostrils
painted red, their marble eyes
startled, distended with effort, their
    jaws carved grimaces of

speed. Round and round go the flying
horses, backs arched in utmost
leaps, necks uptossed or stretched
    out, manes tangled by a wooden

wind. As if lungs of wood inside their
chests pumped, their muscles
heave, and bunch beneath the colored
    traces. Round and round go the flying

horses. Forked in the saddles are thrilled
children, with polished cheeks and fixed
eyes, who reach out in a stretch of
    ambition, leaning out from the turning

pillar. They lean out to snatch the
rings, that are all of wood. But there's one of
brass. All feel lucky as, pass after
    pass, they stay fixed to the flying

horses. The horses' reins and stirrups are
leather. Holes in the rumps spout actual
hair, that hangs to the heels that are held to the
    floor that wobbles around to the reedy

tune. Their tails sweep out on a little
wind, that stirs the grass around the
disk, where the children sit and feel they
    fly, because real wind flies through their

hair. There is one motion and it is
round. There is one music, and its
sound issues from the fulcrum that
    repeats the grainy tune, forever

wound in the flutings of wooden
ears. There is one luck (but it is
rare) that, if you catch, will grant
    release from the circle of the flying

horses. But round and round on the fixed
horses, fashioned to look as if running
races, the children ride as if made of
    wood, till wrinkles carve their smiling

faces, till blindness marbles all their
eyes. Round and round to the sagging
music, the children, all bewitched by their
    greeds, reach out to gather the wooden

rings. And each ring makes a finger
stiff, as oil from the fulcrum blackens the
grass. Round and round go the flying
    hearses, carved and colored to look like steeds.

SWIMMERS

Tossed
by the muscular sea,
we are lost,
and glad to be lost
in troughs of rough

love. A bath in
laughter, our dive
into foam,
our upslide and float
on the surf of desire.

But sucked to the root
of the water-mountain—
immense—
about to tip upon us
the terror of total

delight—
we are towed,
helpless in its
swell, by hooks
of our hair;

then dangled, let go,
made to race—
as the wrestling chest
of the sea, itself
tangled, tumbles

in its own embrace.
Our limbs like eels
are water-boned,
our faces lost
to difference and

contour, as the lapping
crests.
They cease
their charge,
and rock us

in repeating hammocks
of the releasing
tide—
until supine we glide,
on cool green

smiles
of an exhaling
gladiator,
to the shore
of sleep.

THE TALL FIGURES OF GIACOMETTI

We move by means of our mud bumps.
We bubble as do the dead but more slowly.

The products of excruciating purges
we are squeezed out thin hard and dry.

If we exude a stench it is petrified sainthood.
Our feet are large crude fused together

solid like anvils. Ugly as truth is ugly
we are meant to stand upright a long time

and shudder without motion
under the scintillating pins of light

that dart between our bodies
of pimpled mud and your eyes.

THINGS IN COMMON

We have a good relationship, the elevator boy and I.
I can always be cheerful with him.
We make jokes. We both belong to the TGIF Club.
No matter how artificial and stiff I've had to be in the office,
seems like I can be natural with *him*.
We have basic things in common—
the weather, baseball, hangovers,
the superiority of Friday over Monday.

It's true I make it a point to be pleasant to him. Why?
Honest, its because I really like him.
Individually, I mean.
There's something about him—relaxed and balanced
like a dancer or a cat—
as if he knows who he is and where he's at.
At least he knows how to act like that.
Wish I could say the same for myself.

I like his looks, his manner, his red shirt,
the smooth panther shape to his head and neck.
I like it that he knows I don't mean to flirt—
even though I really like him.
I feel he knows I know the score.
It's all in the gleam of his eyes,
the white of his teeth, when he slides back the door
and says, "TGIF, Ma'am, have a nice weekend."

He's strong muscled, good looking—could be 35—
though with his cap off he's 50, I suppose.
So am I. Hope he thinks I look younger too.
I want him to like it that my eyes are blue—

I want him to really like me.
We look straight at each other when we say goodnight.
Is he thinking it's only an accident I'm white?
"TGIF," we say. "Have a nice weekend."

That's the way it's been so far.
We have a good relationship, just the two of us
and the little stool on which he never sits, in the car.
Fridays I work late. I'm the last one down.
Been, let's see, 11 years now. . .
These days I hug the newspaper to me so the headlines won't show.
Why he never has a paper I don't know.
Probably not supposed to read in the elevator.

Lately I've asked myself why don't I say:
"What do you think of the mess down South, Willie?
Or for that matter, right here in D.C.?"
Wish I dared ask him. Or that he'd find a way to put it to me.
I'd like to say bluntly, "Willie, will there be war?"
Neither of us has been able to say it so far.
Will I dare, someday? I doubt it . . . Not *me,* to *him.* . . .
"Thank God It's Friday," we say. "Have a nice weekend."

1.

At moment X
the universe began.
It began at point X.
Since then,
through the Hole in a Nozzle,
stars have spewed. An
inexhaustible gush
populates the void forever.

2.

The universe was there
before time ran.
A grain
slipped in the glass:
the past began.
The Container
of the Stars expands;
the sand
of matter multiplies forever.

3.

From zero radius
to a certain span,
the universe, a Large Lung
specked with stars,
inhales time
until, turgid, it can
hold no more,
and collapses. Then
space breathes, and inhales again,
and breathes again: Forever.

TO MAKE A PLAY

To make a play
is to make people,
to make people do
what you say;

to make real people
do and say
what you make;
to make people make

what you say real;
to make real
people make up
and do what you

make up. What you
make makes people
come and see
what people do

and say, and then
go away and do
what they see—
and see what

they do. Real
people do and say,
and you see and
make up people;

people come to see
what you do.
They see what *they*
do, and they

may go away undone.
You can make
people, or you
can unmake. You

can do or you
can undo. People
you make up make up
and make people;

people come to
see—to see
themselves real,
and they go away

and do what you
say—as if they
were made up,
and wore make-up.

To make a play
is to make
people; to make
people make

themselves; to
make people
make themselves
new. So real.

THE TRUTH

A thick serpent
doubled up with and tangled upon itself.
So twisted, reiterated a heap,
the length and girth and weight appear impossible
to assess.

Speculations about shape amount to a counting
of the coils.

But crawling out or crawling in?

The head is buried
in the muddy middle there.
If that darkest lump *is* a head.
The tail or tails potential everywhere,
cuddled into the interstices.

Part of the difficulty
is the dim light furnished for this
exhibit—
part the heavy glass interposed,
misted with humidities and
exhalations.
All the offal of the opulent awful
occupant on *its* side,
our own smears on ours.

But in the rivet of our stare and vigil
rare satisfaction.
That it exists,
apparently captured,
apparently alive.
Though disinclined to display
any kind of dramatic movement today.

Could we stay till feeding time, indeed there'd be a show.
But no, that's only every thousand years.

A wonder in itself,
and titillation to our fears.

Reluctant mobility,
blunt ambiguity,
indeterminate extent,
obscure function,
undefinable source!

Rigid, yet oozing contradictory power,
the undemonstrative monster roils
our custard-slithery guts.

Sluggish gigantic whip we curse and worship.
Great gray boredom!
When will it lift, strike,
straighten into motion?

UNTITLED

I will be earth you be the flower
You have found my root you are the rain
I will be boat and you the rower
You rock you toss me you are the sea
How be steady earth that's now a flood
The root's the oar's afloat where's blown our bud
We will be desert pure salt the seed
Burn radiant sex born scorpion need

WAKING FROM A NAP ON THE BEACH

Sounds like big
rashers of bacon frying.
I look up from where I'm lying
expecting to see stripes

red and white. My eyes drop shut,
stunned by the sun.
Now the foam is flame, the long
troughs charcoal, but

still it chuckles and sizzles, it
burns and burns, and never gets done.
The sea is that
fat.

THE WATCH

When I
took my
watch to the watchfixer I
felt privileged but also pained to watch the operation. He
had long fingernails and a voluntary squint. He
fixed a magnifying cup over his
squint eye. He
undressed my
watch. I
watched him
split her
in three layers and lay her
middle—a quivering viscera—in a circle on a little plinth. He
shoved shirtsleeves up and leaned like an ogre over my
naked watch. With critical pincers he
poked and stirred. He
lifted out little private things with a magnet too tiny for me
to watch almost. "Watch out!" I
almost said. His
eye watched, enlarged, the secrets of my
watch, and I
watched anxiously. Because what if he
touched her
ticker too rough, and she
gave up the ghost out of pure fright? Or put her
things back backwards so she'd
run backwards after this? Or he
might lose a minuscule part, connected to her
exquisite heart, and mix her
up, instead of fix her.

And all the time,
all the time-
pieces on the walls, on the shelves, told the time,
told the time
in swishes and ticks,
swishes and ticks,
and seemed to be gloating, as they watched and told. I
felt faint, I
was about to lose my
breath—my
ticker going lickety-split—when watchfixer clipped her
three slices together with a gleam and two flicks of his
tools like chopsticks. He
spat out his
eye, lifted her
high, gave her
a twist, set her
hands right, and laid her
little face, quite as usual, in its place on my
wrist.

THE WAVE AND THE DUNE

The wave-shaped dune is still.
Its curve does not break,
though it looks as if it will,

like the head of the dune-
shaped wave advancing,
its ridge strewn

with white shards flaking.
A sand-faced image of the wave
is always in the making.

Opposite the sea's rough glass
cove, the sand's smooth-whittled cave,
under the brow of grass,

is sunny and still. Rushing
to place its replica
on the shore, the sea is pushing

sketches of itself
incessantly into the foreground.
All the models smash upon the shelf,

but grain by grain the creeping sand
reërects their profiles
and makes them stand.

WHILE SEATED IN A PLANE

On a kicked-up floor of cloud
a couch of cloud, deformed and fluffy;
far out, more celestial furniture—fat chairs

slowly puffing forth their airy stuffing.
On dream-feet I walked into that large
parlor on cool pearl—but found it far

between the restless resting places.
Pinnacles, detaching, floating from their bases,
swelled to turbulent beds and tables,

ebbed to ebullient chairs,
then footstools that, degraded,
flowed with the floor before I could get there.

One must be a cloud to occupy a house of cloud.
I twirled in my dream, and was deformed
and reformed, making many faces,

refusing the fixture of a solid soul.
So came to a couch I could believe,
although it altered

its facile carvings, at each heave
became another throne.
Neither dissolved nor solid, I was settled

and unsettled in my placeless chair.
A voluntary mobile, manybodied, I traded
shape for the versatility of air.

A YELLOW CIRCLE

A green
string
is fastened
to the earth,
at its apex
a yellow
circle
of silky
superimposed
spokes.
The sun
is its mother.

Later,
the string
is taller.
The circle
is white—
an aureole
of evanescent
hairs
the wind
makes breathe.

Later still,
it is altered;
the green
string
is thicker,
the white
circle
bald
on one side.
It is a half
circle
the wind lifts away.

Translations of Six Swedish Poets

Ingemar Gustafson (1928-   )

LOCKED IN

All my life I lived in a cocoanut.
It was cramped and dark.
Especially in the morning when I had to shave.
But what pained me most was that I had no way
to get into touch with the outside world.
If no one out there happened to find the cocoanut,
if no one cracked it, then I was doomed
to live all my life in the nut, and maybe even die there.
I died in the cocoanut.
A couple of years later they found the cocoanut,
cracked it, and found me shrunk and crumpled inside.
"What an accident!"
"If only we had found it earlier . . ."
"Then maybe we could have saved him."
"Maybe there are more of them locked in like that . . ."
"Whom we might be able to save,"
they said, and started knocking to pieces every cocoanut
within reach.
No use! Meaningless! A waste of time!
A person who chooses to live in a cocoanut!
Such a nut is one in a million!
But I have a brother-in-law who
lives in an
acorn

UNDER A RAMSHACKLE RAINBOW

A dead tree.
On a rotten branch sit two wingless birds. Among leaves
on the ground a man is searching for his hands.
It is fall.

A stagnant marsh.
On a mossy stone sits the man angling. The hook
is stuck in a waterlily.
The waterlily is stuck in the mud.

An overgrown ruin.
In the grass the man sleeps sitting up. A raindrop descends
in slow-motion through space.
Somewhere in the grass a pike flounders.

A dry well.
At the bottom lies a dead fly. In the wood nearby
a spider gropes through the fog.
The man is trapped in the spiderweb on the horizon.

An abandoned ant hill.
Above a little woodmarsh floats the man. The sun
is just going down. The man has already stopped growing.
The ants gather on the shore.

Werner Aspenström (*1918-*   )

WINTER TALE

I shall never reach your chair
your lips your eyes
those shores I clearly see
infinitely far away
between us the shipwreck in snow.

Yes suddenly the room is full of snow
and suddenly the room is full
of brooding white birds
and soon there is nothing
but silence and sinking islands.
Outside the street's hum is muffled
the trees surrender their outlines
the lanes their cobblestones
the clocks their counting of the hours.
Snow sifts over the room's mirrors
the vase's lilies
the mandolin's strings.
Our feet are rooted and our will
even the longing to travel: between us
a graveyard of snow
for what is not dead but shall be buried.

I shall never reach your chair
your lips your eyes:
Frosty naked walls shall tell
a snow-legend, a winter tale
our shipwreck in crystal.

Eric Lindegren (*1910-*   )

PASTORAL SUITE III

Because our only nest is our wings

    in an air like bluebottle and echoing sea
    in a light of shellshore-colored clouds
    we suddenly hear the evening's whizzing arrow
    we see dusk's double landscape floating

    the bright one in which the mountain seeks it valley
    among the fruits' dawn and the blood's run
    in the hills' roundness like sunfed breasts
    and love's breath on our fields

    the dark one in which the wind drifts its smoke from
    the sorrowful eye of memory, a bell-clang in the distance
    something lost and groping along a root-worn path
    deeper away longer trembling farther away

because our only nest is our wings

    we hear the day's rasp and fruits burst
    we see our shadows redouble and shift

in dusk's flexible flood and foliage
    in the fading thunder's tusk of ivory
    under transparent fragrant tunnels of hay
    in the horizon's thin blade between night and day
    in the sun's red slant and the wash of birdsong
    in the ax-blow that splits and the dusk that floats
    in the bloodbeech's crown where heaven builds its nest
    in the red stream that joins and flows away
    between darkness and dusk that once was light

because our only nest is our wings
  we are suddenly hit by the puff of space
                    and have to scatter
  like dizzyborn foam and racing clouds

  but still we see the earth's dim mirror
  and still we see each other vaguely in its green lake
  like drowned stars we see our limbs glimmer
  and like smoke in storm we see our lips form
  and whirl away and drown—

because our only nest is our wings

  we feel the darkness spread its starsprinkled wings
    to carry away an earth without name

      Oh darkness
      Oh wingslope

  until a last gust of wind throws us deep
                    into each other's arms.

ICARUS

All of it fading now from memory's labyrinth
except the cries that echo there, and the confusion
that arose when he actually swung up from the earth . . .

And how all the clefts that had cried
for their bridges in his breast
slowly came together, like eyelids,
and how the birds brushed past, like shuttles or shots of arrows
until, ultimately, the last lark grazed his hand
and fell away like song.

How he entered the wind's labyrinth, with its blind bulls,
its screams and plunges of light,
its strong dizzying breath, which he long
and laboriously learned to parry,
until again there was focused the bead of his aim and his flight.

Now he soars alone, in a sky without clouds,
in bird-free space among the jet-planes' alarms . . .
rises toward a clearer and clearer sun,
which grows cooler, colder,
up the trajectory of his own freezing blood, and his soul's
fleeing waterfall,

as if enclosed in a speeding shaft,
in an airbubble shooting from the sea's floor to the
enormous magnetic surface:

the birth-sack's explosion transparently near,
the whirl of symbols, freshets, falling azure,
caving walls— and helplessly the cry from the other side:
Reality fallen
of Reality born!

Gunnar Ekelöf (*1907-*   )

AUTUMN TRANCE

Sit still, be silent and wait,
wait for the wildness, for the omen to come,
wait for the marvel, the chaos to come
when time has lost its saltness.
It will streak by with extinguished stars, with whips of comets.
It will come at dawn or at dusk.
Day and night are not its time.
When the sun enters into earth and the moon into stone, it will come
with extinguished stars like burnt-out ships . . .
Then will the blood-gates open, to all
                                                    that is possible.
Then will the bloodless gates close forever.
The ground will shudder with unseen steps, the air
                                                    with unheard sounds.
Towns will collapse punctually as strokes of a gong.
The shells of the ears will burst as if deep under water,
and time's immeasurable numbness be perpetuated
in dead gazes, in jeweled stares
at the marvel brushing past all houses.
Sit still, be silent and wait, breathless
until dawn widens its eye, and breathless until
dusk shuts its lid.

EACH MAN IS A UNIVERSE

Each man is a universe, populated
by blind selves in dark uproar
against the ego, their monarch.
In each self a myriad others crouch,
in each world a myriad others hatch,
and all of them blind. These inner worlds
are real and alive, but unfinished,
as real as I am. And we, monarchs
of a myriad latent selves within,
are blind ourselves, and subject
to some greater Other, whose ego and nature
we as little comprehend as our overself
his Overself. Yet it is their death and their love
that give a tint to our feelings.
As when a great vessel passes at evening
far out, on the rim of the horizon,
and rests there. And we know nothing of it
until a swell from its side reaches the shore,
first one, then another, and many more
that throb and shimmer, until all is calm
as before. Yet everything is different.

So we, the blind, feel a strange craving,
for we sense that our other selves have traveled,
and that among the latent ones, some are at large.

Harry Martinson (1904-   )

HIGH VIEW

These bluish mountains are made of mist and sunsmoke.
Stretch out of yourself, glide suspended
here by the cliff of a mighty cloud.
Here by this mountain which the wind is pushing
ahead of itself, and shifting
to another region,
you can skate out on a mirror of air
to an ocean empty of the ego's island.

Hurry before the guide returns
to label his mountaintop—
before he strenuously starts to sell you
his cliffs and waterfalls.

EVENING INLAND

A silent riddle is reflected. It spins evening
among the still rushes.
There is a gauze that no one notices
in the grass's web.

Silent cattle stare with green eyes,
walking evening-calm to the water down.
And the lake offers to all mouths
its giant spoon.

Karin Boye *(1900-1941)*

ON THE ROAD

The full day is never the great day.
The best day is the day of thirst.

Yes there is goal and purpose to our effort
but the road, the road is our journey's worth.

The best meal is a nightlong rest;
over a little fire, bread broken in haste.

The place slept in only once
is the safest place, with dreams of song.

Break camp, break camp! The big day dawns.
Boundless is our adventure.

YES IT HURTS

Yes it hurts when buds burst.
Why otherwise would spring hesitate?
Why otherwise was all warmth and longing
locked under pale and bitter ice?
The blind bud covered and numb all winter,
what fever for the new compells it to burst?
Yes it hurts when buds burst,
there is pain when something grows
                        and when something must close.

Yes it hurts when the ice drop melts.
Shivering, anxious, swollen it hangs,
gripping the twig but beginning to slip—
its weight tugs it downward, though it resists.
It hurts to be uncertain, cowardly, dissolving,
to feel the pull and call of the depth,
yet to hang and only shiver—
to want to remain, keep firm—
                        yet want to fall.

Then, when it is worst and nothing helps,
they burst, as if in ecstacy, the first buds of the tree,
when fear itself is compelled to let go,
they fall in a glistening veil, all the drops from the twigs,
blinking away their fears of the new,
shutting out their doubts about the journey,
feeling for an instant how this is their greatest safety,
to trust in that daring
                        that shapes the world.